Joseon:

Addressing Unification & Fine Dust

조선 왕조의 수호:통일과 미세먼지 해결.

By Randell Stroud

2021

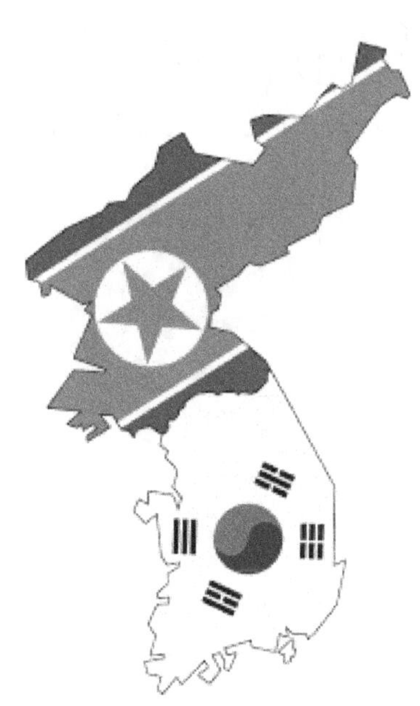

Table of Contents:

Pages 3-5: Introduction

Pages: 6-11- Unification

Page: 12-23: Korea Clean Air Project- Addressing Fine Dust solutions

Introduction:

 You may find it odd that an American has decided to write, publish and submit an essay to the United Nations and to the South Korean Ministry of Environment governmental agency. The reasons are both personal and professional. My reasons are not of self-gain but of pragmatism and of strategy from both a position of global peace keeping and of environmental leadership. Chiefly, these reasons can be summed up into five main categories.

1. Recognizing South Korea's friendship with the United States, a world super-power, the chance of unification between the North and South can create a more powerful ally against other potential foes in the region, acting as a proxy watchmen to US interests. A North/South merger, will create a better standard of life for the people once known under a unified banner of "Joseon" and will result in a more powerful ally to the United States.

2. To honor my grandfather, James Watkins, who fought in the Korean war and to continue his legacy to serve the people of that region and to those who lost their life defending democracy. And to those who endured during the (June Struggle- pro democracy demonstrations) 6월 민주항쟁, who were pivotal in terms of bringing political freedom of choice to the lower peninsula.

3. To take advantage of Korea's leadership in terms of technological advancement in order to encourage surrounding Asiatic nations to take charge in uniting against environmental issues such as "Fine Dust" which is dangerous to health, and to foster friendly relations between the East and West. Such actions could lead to a chain-reaction calling other nations to adopt similar strategies to combat pollution and to peacefully deal with internal strife.

4. To create more political stability in the overall Asiatic region.

5. To bring a sense of aura and peace to the people living near the DMZ.

The Korean peninsula is geographically an interesting place. Below Russia, next to China, above Japan and the Philippines, and among one of (if not the) most technologically advances nations in the world. A perfect blend of conservative family values and progressive technological innovation, this nation stands to be admired by the rest of the world as a shining example. Because of the bloodshed required by Americans to help facilitate such as nation, we owe it to ourselves to not abandon their plight and to commit ourselves to finding diplomatic ways to find routes to unification and to tackle the environmental crisis of Asian Fine Dust, which affects the entire region.

It is my hope, that this report, will encourage Korean, American, and United Nations official to create a coalition with those nations surrounding the Korean Peninsula to combat the fine dust issue, and for the Korean people themselves to see practical reasons behind unification between the North and South. Let us remember, that we too Americans also had a problem between the North and the South, and unification ultimately lead to our nation having increased wealth and military power.

Lastly, I will interject my own innovation, including alternative fuels with a joint venture product invention— Hydrodren as Fuel enhancement, created by a good friend by the name of Dara Cheng, and inventor who has developed a system to double or even triple gas mileage on vehicle while virtually eliminating carbon output.

I pray that this report finds a worthy reader, and such a reader will pass along this report to the proper departments responsible for initiating such an endeavor. I myself, Randell D Stroud, am more than willing to offer my research services or to give any speeches or additional input for potential conferences that may arise from these writings as a result.

With grace and optimism,

Randell D Stroud

Naliniglobalconsulting@gmail.com

Part 1: A case for Unification & Restoration of Joseon :
조선의 수복과 통일을 위한 사례.

In recent years, the U.S. has refused to relax economic sanctions against North Korea. South Korean president, Moon Jae-in, had previously pressed for the easing of such restrictions and sought to resume stalled inter-Korean economic projects such as a joint factory park and mountain resort. Former U.S. President Donald Trump opposed a request by South Korean President Moon Jae-in to resume economic cooperation with North Korea at a summit on June 30 2019, the Yomiuri newspaper reported.

More than half of South Korea's university-age students now possess a positive view toward Korean unification. That's according to a new poll conducted by the National Assembly's Foreign Affairs and Unification Committee. The survey was conducted in early November, canvassing more than 1,000 university students nationwide. Unification of South and North Korea presents many challenges beyond ideological differences.

Economic Consequences: South Korea's GDP is many times multiplied over its North Korean Counterpart. The gross domestic product (GDP) of North Korea is estimated to be $40 billion in 2015, according to the CIA's World Fact-book, which has not given any updated GDP information since that date. In terms of GDP per capita, North Korea had a per capita GDP of $1,700. The South Korean FDP is estimated to be over 1.531 trillion USD (2017).

If unification took place, the South Korean portion of the peninsula would be largely responsible for developing its Northern counterpart, although on a plus side, the North Koreans have a vast military and its own natural resources. In due time, it could supply the South Koreans with many benefits. It's a short term cost versus a long term investment.

Political Involvement: If Korea returned to its former empire of the Joseon Kingdom, who would be its ruler? Kim Jong Un or Moon Jae-In? This would arguably be the largest hurdle. The people of both North and South Korea would have to hold a new election in order to bring in a fresh new government. Would the government be capitalist or communist in nature? Would both leaders be willing to give up their own power in order to bring about unification?

 Foreign Influence: If you study the history of Korea (Joseon Kingdom), you will quickly learn that the North and South are merely consequences of the Cold War between Russia and the United States. After the end of WW2, Russia (then USSR) and the USA, divided Korean ownership into two nation states. Much like what happened in Germany and Vietnam. Balancing national sovereignty and independence while still maintaining a respectful level of guardianship over interests and investments following such proxy wars, is quite difficult.

In a sense, the Korean struggle is a proxy war between the USA and communist Russia. Until the Korean people realize that they are essentially puppets of the old USSR and modern United States of America, they will fail to see the con-artistry that was placed upon their brethren. If the North and South unite, they will arguably be one of the most powerful nations in the world. This is contrary to the interests of China, Russia, and the United States. Many of these so called "peace-talks", are merely for show, and the Koreans must be privy to this.

Assimilation: Once unification happens, many North Koreans will migrate to the south since it is more economically sound than the north. How will the economy absorb this? How will the culture be affected on a local scale? How will society integrate them? Many reports already show North Koreans being discriminated against in the southern regions due to them being far behind in terms of education and physical health. How will North Korea's military weapons and natural resources be combined with South Korea's military power and natural resources?

Cooperation from Foreign countries: China, Russia, and the United States all have an economic and political stake in the Korean Peninsula. All three countries must be on board with this assimilation. By combining both Northern and Southern provinces, the peninsula could theoretically obtain vast powers that could rival China, Russia, and the United States. Just as President Moon has recently attempted to create a joint business venture with Chairman Kim in the form of a joint factor and vacation resort transcending the DMZ, American President Donald Trump, blocked such a measure stating that North Korea must agree to reduce its nuclear program even more so.

We must trust South Koreans in their attempts to negotiate with North Koreans. The United States, Russia, and China must all work together by taking a step back and allowing the people of both North and South Korea to negotiate their own affairs. Sometimes, doing less is akin to doing more. President Moon and Chairman Kim must take more initiative in negotiating the sovereignty of their kinship by relying less on foreign powers; specifically Russia, China, and the United States. Nobody knows the Korean people better than those who speak the language and live in the culture of the Korean peninsula formerly known as "Joseon".   The Koreans of both the North and South have far more to gain than the Russians, Chinese, and Americans have to lose by initiating unification. The prospect of peace and prosperity outweigh any risks of collapse, as it is in the interest of the world for unification to be successful.

My grandfather, SGT James Edwards Watkins of the US Army, fought in the Korean War, who is now deceased, fought to see a unified Korea. Economically, politically, and socially, it would not be an easy task, however, in the spirit of freedom and liberty, I believe that perhaps after 10 or 20 years post-unification, Korea could very well become the most powerful nation in the Asiatic region and quite possible become a beacon of hope in terms of pro-democracy, economic stability, free-speech, technological advancement and a positive example to all countries within close proximity to the region including the South-East Asian nations including Malaysia, Thailand, and Indo-Filipino islands.

Through localization of alliances and communications within the east and southeast regions of Asia, I believe that the Korea peninsula can become a shining example of social/economic prosperity and responsible power. Militarily and natural resource wise, North Korea is quite capable, alas, socially and economically, South Korea has much more to offer. If both regions were to successfully reunite, I truly believe that the region could become a leader in the United Nation Security Council and perhaps replace China as one of the "P-5" nations appointed to the UN on foreign affairs or through special vote, become an added addition. The Korean peninsula is unique in the sense of its economic and military power. Under the right circumstances, I believe that this unification could create a new force in the region that could fundamentally preserve peace, prosperity, and human rights.

The sinful karma of the Cold War must be accounted for. The sins of the past, if healed correctly could restore the former honor of Korea as it once held prior to the Japanese invasion of 1910. North Koreans and South Koreans have one thing in common, they are Koreans! They speak the same language, and have the same blood coursing through their veins. They must no longer allow themselves to continue being the consequence of the Cold War between Russia and the USA. Until both the North and South Koreans can realize that they are merely puppets to foreign forces, they will be blinded by their own selfish ambitions and never truly realize the power they are capable of as a shared race of people.

To the people of Korea, I say to you, 감사합니다 (thank you), for listening to the words of a humble Migukin (American), who truly loves, respects, and admires the resolve of the Kingdom of JOSEON. Please continue to fight for the sovereignty and prosperity of your land, absence of undue foreign influence or manipulation. Take charge of your bloodline and reclaim the title of a unified people! Only the Korean people can solve the problems of the Korean people. The Americans, the Russians, and the Chinese are merely advocates or enemies to overcome. I can't speak for the Chinese or Russians, but it's safe to say that Korea and the United States will always have a special friendship. In the end, it is up to the Korean people to realize the strength and beauty of a reunited culture that will be soon known as the restored Kingdom of Joseon. As a result, renewed confidence and peace will be established in the region, and the US can let rest its arms, and let the locals take more reign over their future.

PART 2: ASIAN FINE DUST—PROJECT- KOREA CLEAN AIR ACTION (한국 청정 대기 행동) by

Randell Stroud

Table of Contents:

I: Problem Introduction

II: History of yellow dust & fine dust

III. Solutions

I. Introduction:

 This report will attempt to explain the environmental issues facing the Korean peninsula in regards to the "fine dust" or "yellow dust" phenomena which effects the health of Koreans on an annual bases for days, weeks, or even sometimes months at a time. In this report, we will discuss the history behind these environmental events, its causes, and possible solutions. "Fine Dust" or "Yellow Dust", refer to harmful particulates found in the air stemming from the deserts of Mongolia and west China. Pollutants coming from domestic and foreign man-made sources from factories, combustion engines, methane gases, and refineries will also be considered.

II. History.

"Fine Dust" or "Asian Dust" , affects much of East Asia all-year round but especially during the months of March, April, and May. The yellow tinted particulates derive from the deserts of Mongolia, China and Kazakhstan, where high-speed surface winds and severe dust storms, push sand particles into the atmosphere . These "Sand clouds" are then pushed eastward by wind currents that pass over China, North and South Korea,Japan, and Eastern Russia. On rare occasion, the particulates are carried as far as the western coast of California, affecting the air quality there to a certain degree.

In recent years, it has become a serious problem due to the increasing industrialization of China and Korea, factories and refineries spew pollutants that mix with the dust coming from the deserts of China. This combination has been causing more frequent occurrences of the fine-dust phenomena. In the last few decades the Aral Sea of Kazakhstan and Uzbekistan have began drying up due to the diversion of the Amu River and Syr River following a Soviet agricultural program to irrigate Central Asian deserts, mainly for cotton plantations.

Recently, it has been discovered that yellow dust consists of fine dust and ultrafine dust particles.[1] Fine dust consists of fine particular matter (PM). Particles smaller than 10μm in diameter are classified as fine PM (PM10), while particles smaller than 2.5μm in diameter are classified as ultrafine PM (PM2.5). Both fine and ultrafine dust particles impose dangers to health. Fine dust particles are small enough to penetrate deep into the lung alveoli. Ultrafine dust particles are so small that after they also penetrate into the blood or lymphatic system through the lungs. Once in the bloodstream, ultrafine particles can even reach the brain or fetal organs. "– From Wikipedia with sources". According to an article written by the US National Library of Medicine…..

National Institutes of Health,   ---- "Estimation of the effects of heavy Asian dust on respiratory function by definition type" , showed a direct correlation between respiratory problems and fine dust, especially on days with heavy particulate readings.

As illustrated in the report, "Socio-Economic Costs from Yellow Dust Damages in South Korea" by Dai-Yeun Jeong, states that, "……Socio-economic Cost Estimated by Contingent Valuation Method. Kang et al. (2004) estimated the socio-economic cost assuming that yellow dust occurs an average 14 days per year. They first estimated the socio-economic cost per person, and multiplied this for the whole population and total cost ; the cost was estimated as US$29.51 per person a year. Multiplied by total number of people in Korea an estimated cost of US$ 44.123 million results. The total socio-economic cost is then estimated as US$ 5,921.639 million when a discount rate of 7.5% is applied."

Not only does the Asian dust crisis affect the economy and the health of Korean citizens, but also on the marine life in the oceans surrounding the Korean peninsula. According to a study published by Sciencedaily.com — " East Asian dust deposition impacts on marine biological productivity" December 6, 2016–" — the article states, "…Results showed that dust containing iron was the most important factor affecting phytoplankton growth and the deposition of iron via severe dust storms satisfied the increase in demand required for phytoplankton growth (115-291%), followed by nitrogen (it accounted for up to 1.7-4.0%), and phosphorus was the smallest one (it accounted for up to 0.2-0.5%)."

Now that we have a basic understanding and what factors are causing this natural disaster, compounded by man-made waste, we must now ask ourselves, "What can be done about it?"

Solutions:

In January of 2019, President Moon Jae-in, announced, South Korea will produce 6.2 million units of fuel cell electric vehicles and build 1,200 refilling stations across the country by 2040 as an effort to create more sustainable energy and less pollution in the nation. According to the article, "Seoul's Answer to a Pollution Crisis: Free Public Transit" by Linda Poon, JAN 24, 2018, Alongside this push as part of an emergency plan announced last year by Seoul Mayor Park Won-soon, the city will make public transit free during rush hours on days when the air quality index reaches above 50 and is expected to stay there for at least a day. To fund the measure, Park set aside 24.9 billion won (about $23 million USD) in December, stating that the air quality had turned into a natural disaster which warranted access to use emergency disaster relief revenue.

Last month, Thailand began deploying manned drones to spraying water into the air in an effort to clear the debris. The degree of success from these results are unknown, but I assume them to be of little value considering no public reports being issued stating any major improvements. Thai authorities announced on Jan.24, 2019, that they have arrested the operator of a website that may have falsely claimed that a woman had died as a result of a small "PM 2.5" particulate matter that experts say is one of the most dangerous constituents of air pollution because it can penetrate deep into the lungs. With the rise of COVID-19 infections, this combination could prove even more disastrous if not handled in a timely fashion.

Although COVID-19 is not statistically a dangerous disease, especially for the young and healthy, aggravating factors such as the fine dust issue could affect those mortality rates in a negative way. Alas, this issue has many contributing factors.

Chinese industrialization is often cited as a reason for increased fine dust occurrences. Per *Tradingeconomics.com– National Bureau of Statistics China* – Show massive amounts of increased industrialization from 1990-2015, whereas production has recently began to level out. China's population of 1.4 billion people is also of significance. Some claim China's firework displays during the Lantern Festival and stagnant air over the Korean peninsula are the main culprits for the dangerously high levels of ultra-fine dust pollution in South Korea at the end of February, a Seoul City-run environment agency said on Wednesday (March 6). -"High density of ultra-fine dust continued recently because the weather condition caused air over the Korean peninsula to be stagnant and delayed diffusion of pollutants stemming within the country and from abroad," said Mr Shin Yong-seung of the Research Institute of Public Health and Environment." -The agency traced the chemical elements travelling from China to South Korea on two occasions – from Feb 17 to Feb 23 and from Feb 27 to Tuesday. (Source: Korea Herald)

"In order to combat this issue, we must use a combination of natural, political, and technological means." – Randell Stroud

Plant based city-wide filtration via a "Green initiative" with a new city planning development project which will envelop the city rooftops and intersections with certain plants known to filter toxins in the air.

Switch Korean vehicles from combustion based to election based by the year 2040.

Pass regulations requiring manufacturers to install and maintain all filtration, boilers, and equipment in their facilities in order to reduce emissions.

Hold an east Asian convention compelling afflicted nations to take measures in combating Asian dust. Mongolia, China, Russia, South/North Korea.

In phase #1, I am inspired by the NASA clean air study regarding plant life. The Clean Air study found that English Ivy, The Snake Plant, the Peace Lily, and several other plants are very effective at removing benzene, formaldehyde, and trichloroethylene, xylene, and ammonia from the air—chemicals that have been linked to health effects like headaches and eye irritation. Urban areas like Seoul, and Gangnam, are full of empty rooftops which could be fitted with these plants. Sidewalks, highways, and intersections could also be equipped with plant life to filter out these toxins. The study found that a single tree could potentially filter out a 100 sq ft radius. These plants collect the dust, filter the air, and hold onto the dust, only to be washed away by a rainy day at a later time. The effects will be subtle at first, but can be dramatic as the project grows. Koreans will certainly feel the difference even by affixing these plants into their living-rooms at home.

(Sidenote: -President Moon and other leaders could potentially create a huge public works project, employing citizens to plant and maintain this project which would also create thousands of jobs of unemployed or semi-retired Koreans. Since this is an international issue, funds could be gathered via taxation, international relief funds, and by a global public announcement campaign championing for voluntary donations.)

In phase#2, President Moon has already done a fantastic job in pushing for an alternative to combustion vehicles. By 2040, if South Korea sees a switch from combustion to electric, particulate levels are certain to decrease by a large degree. With the rise of the Tesla Corporation in the west, the practicality and popularity of this idea is growing rapidly. However, resources needed to create lithium or otherwise mineral based electric batteries are not without environmental concerns, especially in terms of disposal. This is why I am an advocate for the products created by Dara Cheng, a Cambodian-American, and CEO of "Nature & Technology". We have consulted together many times in production and design in regards to a converter box which allows modern engines to run on an oxygen/hydrogen based system, which doubles or even triples fuel economy in many cases while virtually eliminating 99.9% of carbon emissions by fully burning this type of fuel, eliminating the need of catalytic converters, which will also bring the cost of automobiles down for consumers and manufactures. Traditional fuel would only be needed as a primer in conjunction with this technology, thus resulting in sharp decreases in consumption of non-renewable resources.

This is a product that I am pushing and hope will soon be presented to Hyundai or other Korean based corporations who appear to be friendlier towards new technology. Alas, only time will tell, and due to economic pressures and patents pending, business dealings are almost always on a first-come basis. After Mr. Cheng, presented me with a presentation on his technologies, and with my legal/business acumen, we hope to join forces and convince world-wide adaptation of this technology which will greatly impact the reduction of harmful NOX gases and harmful particulates from damaging the lungs of our fellow human beings. These matters are all pending at the moment, but present an interesting conversation to be had.

In phase #3, inspectors must hold corporations to a higher standard in both China and Korea. Boiler-makers and other filtration systems that are not properly maintained have been shown to increase air pollution and reduce productivity of equipment. By not properly maintaining these facilities or by failing to upgrade outdated technologies, companies suffer economically due to equipment stagnation, and the people of China and Korea suffer environmentally and biologically.

In phase #4, we have to build a coalition that includes China, Russia, Mongolia, and both North and South Korea. By agreeing to mutual regulations, combining incomes and efforts of scientists, political sanctions and talks of aggression can be mitigated by a mutual desire to have clean air for their respective citizen to enjoy. Cross-contamination/pollutants caused by neighboring countries must be addressed in a friendly dialogue in order to establish a sense of brotherhood.

No single country can be blamed for this environmental crisis as all nations contribute to harmful particulates being found in the air, whereas we must all be willing to contribute and do our parts.

This report is simplistic and indirect, but points us in the right direction. Collaborative and creative methods are a winning combination that are sure to yield results. If President Moon Jae-in, Chairman Kim Jong-Un, Prime Minister Ukhnaagiin Khürelsükh of Mongolia, President Vladamir Putin, and President Xi Jinping, are willing to organize a coalition, Randell Stroud and his colleagues will volunteer its research efforts towards this project.

Sincerely,

Randell D Stroud,

Human rights specialist/Paralegal

Naliniglobalconsulting@gmail.com

Division of Environmental Law and Conventions

P.O Box 30552, 00100

Nairobi, Kenya

Fax: +254 20 7624300

E-mail Address: delc@unep.org

Ministry of Environment South Korea:

Government Complex-Sejong, 11, Doum 6-Ro, Sejong-si, 30103, Republic of Korea: E-mail address: mepr@korea.kr

Dedication:

**(To my Grandfather and adopted Uncle—Circa Korean
War- who fought for freedom and democracy- may
their sacrifices not be in vain)**

Notes:

Contact:

Randell D Stroud

Naliniglobalconsulting@gmail.com

615-891-0476

www.ingramcontent.com/pod-product-compliance
Lightning Source LLC
Chambersburg PA
CBHW061326250726
48657CB00003B/1060